D1338468

EDITED BY HELEN EXLEY
ILLUSTRATED BY JULIETTE CLARKE

Published simultaneously in 1999 by Exley Publications Ltd in Great
Britain, and Exley Publications LLC in the USA.
Copyright © Helen Exley 1999
The moral right of the author has been asserted.

12 11 10 9 8 7 6 5 4 3 2 1

ISBN 1-86187-122-8

Printed in China.
Exley Publications Ltd, 16 Chalk Hill, Watford, Herts WD1 4BN, UK.
Exley Publications LLC, 232 Madison Avenue, Suite 1206, NY 10016, U

The publishers are grateful for permission to reproduce copyright material. Whilst eve
reasonable effort has been made to trace copyright holders, the publishers would be
pleased to hear from any not here acknowledged. HAROLD MONRO: From "Milk F
The Cat". Reprinted with permission of Gerald Duckworth and Company Ltd.
RUDYARD KIPLING: From "The Just So Stories". Reprinted with permission of A. P
Watt Ltd on behalf of The National Trust for Places of Historic Interest or Natural Bea

EXLEY
NEW YORK · WATFORD, UK

THE LITTLEST
Cat
BOOK

A HELEN EXLEY GIFTBOOK

A morning kiss, a discreet touch of his nose landing somewhere on the middle of my face. Because his long white whiskers tickled, I began every day laughing.

JANET F. FAURE

EVERYBODY LOVES HIM,

AND HE, PERFECTLY

AMICABLY, LOVES

NOTHING EXCEPT HIMSELF.

MELISSA JONES, AGE 12

While still a kitten, all fluff and buzzes, Pete had worked out a simple philosophy. I was in charge of quarters, rations and weather; he was in charge of everything else.

ROBERT HEINLEIN, FROM "THE DOOR INTO SUMMER"

ONE
SMALL CAT
CHANGES
COMING HOME
TO AN
EMPTY HOUSE TO
COMING HOME.

PAM BROWN, b.1928

A cat does not leap up at you,
or lick your face all over
or run mad circles round you,
making hysterical noises.
It meets you at the door
and leans very softly against
your legs and reverberates.

PAM BROWN, b.1928

A cat's purr — kitchen,
tabby or tiger — is the most
contented sound on earth.

PAM BROWN, b.1928

... it was difficult to feel
vexed by a creature
that burst into a chorus of
purring as soon as I spoke
to him.

PHILIP BROWN

Like those great
sphinxes lounging
through eternity in
noble attitudes upon
the desert sand,
they gaze incuriously at
nothing, calm and wise.

CHARLES BAUDELAIRE
(1821-1867)

...*When she walked*... *she stretched out
long and thin like a little tiger,
and held her head high to look over
the grass as if she were threading
the jungle.*

SARAH ORNE JEWETT (1849-1909)

*In Ancient Egypt
they were worshipped
as gods.
This makes them too prone
to set themselves up as critics
and censors of the frail
and erring human beings
whose lot they share.*

P.G. WODEHOUSE
(1881-1975)

Sometimes he will sit in front of you with eyes so melting, so caressing and so human, that they almost frighten you, for it is impossible to believe that a soul is not there.

THEOPHILE GAUTIER (1811-1872)

I love cats. I love their
grace and their elegance.
I love their independence
and their arrogance, and
the way they lie and look at
you, summing you up...
with that unnerving,
unwinking, appraising
stare.

JOYCE STRANGER, FROM "KYM"

A cat or dog does not help
merely by being soft and
warm and alive, but by
telling the human being
that it does not matter
if she or he is old or ugly,
helpless or confused.

It does not matter that they have failed, if they are poor, or that the world seems to have no further use for them. An animal sees the self that has never changed since it was new born, the young soul that occupies the old or injured body.

PAM BROWN, b.1928

He lies there, purring and
dreaming, shifting his limbs
now and then in an ecstasy
of cushioned comfort.
He seems the incarnation
of everything soft and silky
and velvety, without a sharp
edge in his composition,
a dreamer....

SAKI (1870-1916)

Juliette Clarke

... when Agrippina has breakfasted, and washed, and sits in the sunlight blinking at me with affectionate contempt, I feel soothed by her absolute and unqualified enjoyment... for her, time and the world hold only this brief moment of contentment.

AGNES REPPLIER

*If there is just
one beam of
sunshine coming
into a room
you can be sure
that the cat is
lazing in its heat.*

STUART AND LINDA
MACFARLANE

DOGS HAVE OWNERS.
CATS HAVE SLAVES.

AMANDA BELL

A cat isn't fussy — just so long as you remember he likes his milk in the shallow rose-patterned saucer and his fish on the blue plate. From which he will take it, and eat it off the floor.

ARTHUR BRIDGES

Cats try to teach their humans a few basic words of cat language. They find that most humans can learn simple phrases such as "Let me out", "You're an idiot", "I want some dinner" and "Play with me."

STUART AND LINDA MACFARLANE

Given a houseful of
carpets, shelves, cushions,
chairs, window sills,
any cat will choose
to sleep on the document
you are using.

DOMINIC COURCEL

A kind cat likes
to lend a hand
with casting on,
casting off,
wrapping parcels,
writing essays,
sorting papers,
making beds and
hanging out
the washing.

PAM BROWN, b. 1928

Cat's Daily Task List

00:00–07:00 Sleep on bed
07:00–07:10 Breakfast
07:10–12:00 Sleep on chair
12:00–12:10 Lunch
12:10–15:00 Sleep on top of refrigerator
15:00–15:01 Exercise (optional)
15:01–18:00 Sleep under heater
18:00–18:15 Dinner
18:15–00:00 Sleep in drawer

STUART AND LINDA MACFARLANE

Every cat in the area will come round to try out your new cat flap. Your own cat will continue to climb onto the window ledge and demand that you get out of bed to let it in.

BRIAN KING

Watch your kitten make a snug home for itself in a shoe-box. Two weeks later, see the outrage on his face. "This shoe-box has shrunk! I am being forced to live in an Unfair World!"

CHRISTINE HARRIS

To satisfy a cat a new state of
being needs to be created –
halfway between in and out.

STUART AND LINDA MACFARLANE

Cats hate a closed door...
regardless of which side
they're on.

LILIAN JACKSON BRAUN

DOGS COME WHEN THEY ARE CALLED; CATS TAKE A MESSAGE AND GET BACK TO YOU.

MARY BLY

*No one ever owned
a cat.*

PAM BROWN, b.1928

*You don't train cats.
They train you.*

ALLEN AND IVY DODD

Cats have very small vocabularies. They don't see why they should waste time learning words.
After all — they have no intention of obeying anyone.

CHARLOTTE GRAY

What are little kittens
made of?
30% cuteness
29% mischief
28% purrs
10% soft fur
3% innocence

LISETTE FAVIER

IF CATS RULED THE WORLD:

Dogs would have to
curtsey or bow
when a cat went past.
Tom and Jerry cartoons
would be shown on TV
twenty-four hours a day.

Cream
would be available
"on tap".
Their human would be in
attendance at all times.
Mice would be available
in a variety of tastes.
Rain would be abolished.

STUART AND LINDA MACFARLANE

BEING ADOPTED BY A STRAY CAT
IS A SIGN THAT YOU ARE A KIND,
GENEROUS, WARM-HEARTED
SUCKER.

GIOVANNI ANDRETTI

CATS HAVE NIGHTMARES ABOUT:
Being chased by mice the size of dogs.
Life number ten.
Being bathed in soapy water then
covered in flea powder.

Work.
Being laughed at for getting stuck
up a tree.
Turning into a dog.

STUART AND LINDA MACFARLANE

You can feel an awful fool standing at the bottom of the garden yelling pussy, pussy, pussy across a totally deserted meadow. Especially when you realise that pussy, pussy, pussy is watching you, with benign interest, from the shelter of the garden shed.

MARCIA FISCHER

Cats like to lie and listen
to you calling.
When discovered, they are
indignant "Me? I never knew
you meant me!"

PAM BROWN, b.1928

... and when the moon gets up and night comes, he is the Cat that walks by himself, and all places are alike to him. Then he goes out to the Wet Wild Woods or up on the Wet Wild Trees or on the Wet Wild Roofs, waving his wild tail and walking by his wild lone.

RUDYARD KIPLING (1865-1936),
FROM "JUST SO STORIES"

Give her but a wavering leaf-shadow of a breeze combing the grasses and she was back a million years, glaring with night-lit eyes in the thickets, projecting a terrible aura of fear that stilled and quelled all creatures.

PAUL ANNIXTER

A cat, with its phosphorescent eyes that shine like lanterns, and sparks flashing from its back, moves fearlessly through the darkness....

THEOPHILE GAUTIER

Juliette Clarke

At first she pretends,
having nothing to do,
She has come in merely
to blink by the grate,
But, though tea may be late
or the milk may be sour,
She is never late.

HAROLD MONRO,
FROM "MILK FOR THE CAT"

As to sagacity, I should
say that his judgement
respecting the warmest
place and the softest
cushion in a room is
infallible...

THOMAS HENRY HUXLEY

He is excessively proud, and, when he is made the subject of conversation, will cast one glance of scorn, and leave the room...

ANDREW LANG (1844-1912)

If cats could talk, they
would lie to you.

ROB KOPACK

Do not attempt to teach your cats tricks – they already know every trick there is.

SIDRA MALIK

When a stray cat visits your house he will appear curious. What he is actually doing is examining the accommodation and interviewing you as his prospective new human. If the house has suitable

cozy places and you appear to be able to keep him in the high standard of living to which he is aspiring he may decide to adopt you.

STUART AND LINDA MACFARLANE

A cat will vividly enact the chase
with a dry leaf as a mouse
— until some silly human being says,
"Kill it," then "Kill the mouse!"
When he will stare in disdain,
"Mouse? For heavens sake,
can't you see it's a dead leaf!"

PAM BROWN, b.1928

Kittens and
curtains.
One must
choose
which one loves
most.

PAM BROWN, b.1928

Cats most-liked places to sharpen
their claws:
1) New wallpaper
2) Antique and expensive furniture
3) Silk stockings
4) Your best clothes
5) Your new suite

JAMES GIBSON

We got her a scratch pad
but she likes the chair better.

ALASTAIR GOODMAN, AGE 9

Can't find the cat? Try to quietly open a tin of salmon and you will find her right by your side.

STUART AND LINDA MACFARLANE

... Cats only occupy space and think about three things: food, sex and nothing. If they're neutered that leaves food.

PENNY WARD MOSER

A hungry cat outperforms the loudest alarm clock.

LI MING JIN

A kitten
is a lethal weapon
disguised as
a cute fluffy bundle
of joy.

STUART AND LINDA MACFARLANE

A kitten is… mischief in mink.

CHRISTINE HARRIS

My pet wears small white socks.
She's a crafty old thing is my
little pet. She flicks her paw in
and out of the fish bowl.
She's frightened of getting her
little white socks wet but I know
she'd love to grab him.

MAUREEN MCGINLEY, AGE 12

*A*bout a year ago I won some goldfish at a fair but guess who ate them!

LOUISE ALLISON, AGE 10

When my cats aren't happy,
I'm not happy... because I know
they're just sitting there
thinking up ways to get even.

PENNY WARD MOSER

Only cat lovers know the luxury of fur-coated, musical hot water bottles that never go cold.

SUSANNE MILLEN

Never belittle the comfort offered by a cat — she has no words, but by small touchings and buttings and leanings, she shows her love for you — and tries to distract you from your sorrow.

PAM BROWN, b.1928

At intervals the cat rouses
you to reassure you of its love
by putting its paw in your eye,
your nostrils, your mouth.
It pats your face with gently
extended claws, breathes in
your ear, combs your hair,
butts you with its rock hard
skull. Or smothers you softly
in a luxury of fur.

CHARLOTTE GRAY

A quiet child, a trusting
kitten, a garden peppery
with the scent of lupins.
Of these simple ingredients
are the memories made
which return years later,
bringing tears to the eyes.

CHRISTINE HARRIS

*We've got each other trained
— cat and I.
I want to play — he looks
indignant.
I want to watch TV — he
demands to play.
I open the door to let him out
— he changes his mind.*

I close the door again — he
makes a dash to get out.
I serve his dinner — he turns
away in disgust.
I serve my dinner — he
demands to be fed.
Yes, we have an understanding
— cat and I.

STUART AND LINDA MACFARLANE

*... rejoicing in shared, simple
pleasures.
Leaning together in drowsy
contentment.
Talking wordlessly in purrs and
murmurings.
Delighting in fire, in sunlight.*

*Amusing each other with small
silliness.
Relishing food.
Happy in one another's company.*

CHARLOTTE GRAY

With a cat there is out time
and food time and doze time
and play time
– and a time given over
entirely to slosh.
Nose against nose, face
against face,
pattings and snugglings and
rapturous purrings
And a cuddling down to sleep.

PAM BROWN, b.1928